915.61
MIT
C.96

Mitten, Christopher.

Turkey.

$31.43

34880030037696

DATE			

Steadwell Books World Tour

TURKEY

CHRISTOPHER MITTEN

Steadwell Books

Raintree Steck-Vaughn Publishers
A Harcourt Company

Austin · New York
www.raintreesteckvaughn.com

Copyright © 2002 Steck-Vaughn Company

Published by Raintree Steck-Vaughn Publishers, an imprint of Steck-Vaughn Company

Editor: Simone T. Ribke
Designer: Maria E. Torres

Library of Congress Cataloging-in-Publication Data
Mitten, Christopher.
    Turkey / Christopher Mitten.
        p. cm. -- (Steadwell books world tour)
    Summary: Describes the history, geography, economy, government, religious and social life, language and culture, various famous people, and outstanding tourist sites of Turkey. Includes a recipe for Turkish lemonade.
    ISBN 0-7398-5757-6
        1. Turkey--Description and travel. [1. Turkey.] I. Title. II. Series.

    DR429.4 .M58 2002
    915--dc21   2002017869

Printed in the United States of America
1 2 3 4 5 6 7 8 9 10 WZ 07 06 05 04 03 02

Photo acknowledgments
Cover (a) ©Steve Vidler/SuperStock; cover (b) ©Steve Vidler/eStock; cover (c) ©Robert Frerck/Odyssey/Chicago; p.1a ©Walter Bibikow/The Viesti Collection, Inc.; p.1b ©Jeff Greenberg/Visuals Unlimited; p.1c ©Steve Vidler/eStock; p.3a ©Robert Frerck/Odyssey/ Chicago; p.3b ©Walter Bibikow/The Viesti Collection, Inc.; p.5 ©Nik Wheeler/CORBIS; p.6 ©Steve Vidler/eStock; p.7 ©G Spenceley/TRIP; p.8 ©Walter Bibikow/The Viesti Collection, Inc; p.13 ©Steve Vidler/SuperStock; p.14 ©Atlas Geographic Magazine; p.15 ©Adam Woolfitt/ CORBIS; p.16 ©Walter Bibikow/The Viesti Collection, Inc.; p.21a ©Robert Frerck/Odyssey/Chicago; p.21b ©AFP/CORBIS; p.25a ©Adam Woolfitt/CORBIS; p.26a ©Jose F. Poblete/CORBIS; p.26b ©Walter Bibikow/The Viesti Collection, Inc.; p.28 ©Barry Iverson/TimePix; p.29 ©Chris Hellier/CORBIS; p.31a ©Maury Englander/SuperStock; p.31b ©Robert Frerck/Odyssey/Chicago; p.34 ©Brauner/StockFood; p.37a,b ©Jeff Greenberg/Visuals Unlimited; p.38 ©Atlas Geographic Magazine; p.40 ©Kate Clow/TRIP; p.41 ©Jeff Greenberg/Visuals Unlimited; p.42,43b ©Walter Bibikow/The Viesti Collection, Inc.; p.44a ©Burnhan Ozbici/AP/Wide World Photos; p.44b ©Bettmann/CORBIS; p.44c ©Atlas Geographic Magazine.

Additional Photography by Corbis Royalty Free, Getty Images Royalty Free, and the Steck-Vaughn Collection.

CONTENTS

Welcome to Turkey

Do you want to learn something about Turkey? The best way is to go there. Traveling through its ancient cliffside villages, swimming on its sandy shores, and experiencing the excitement of its cities will teach you all about this incredible nation. Turkey's colorful cities and dramatic landscapes make for great reading. So whether you want to visit, or just want to learn something about a far-off land, read on. Turkey is waiting!

Pronunciation Guide

Hittite	HIH-tite
Byzantine	BIH-zen-teen
Seljuk	sel-JOOK
Dolmamabahçe	DOLH-muh BAH-chay
Abdül Mecit	AHB-dohl may-JEET
Balîk	BAH-lihk
Üsküdar	OOS-kuh-dar
Büyük Çamlica	BUH-yuhk Chuhm-lih-jah
Ankara	ON-kuh-ruh
Nemrut Dagi	nehm-RUHT Dah-ih
Hattuøa	hah-TOO-shah
Aslanîî	AHS-lah-niih
Kapî	KAH-pih

▲ **TOMBS OF DALYAN**
These tombs were built for Turkish kings in the 4th century. Take a boat ride to get a better view.

TURKEY'S PAST

Turkey's history is filled with wonderful stories. From ancient Hittites to powerful **sultans**, Turkey's past makes for great reading.

Ancient History

The oldest settlements in Turkey date back 10,000 years. Turkey's first major civilization was the Hittite **Empire**, from 2600 to 1200 B.C. It was well-known for its gold jewelry, sculptures, and pottery.

Around 1200 B.C., other peoples began to invade Turkey. The Persians were the most successful. But in 334 B.C., Alexander the Great conquered Turkey for Greece. Later, Turkey fell into the hands of the Roman Empire.

A Roman emperor named Constantine, whose rule began in A.D. 324, changed history by becoming Christian. He helped the Christian religion spread all over the world by allowing freedom of religion in his empire.

Constantine made a Turkish capital within the Roman Empire. This city was first called Constantinople. Much later, its name was changed to Istanbul. It is Turkey's largest **metropolis**.

◀ **THE TROJAN HORSE**
The Greeks gave a huge wooden horse to the city of Troy in Turkey—but it was a trick gift. Greek soldiers were hidden inside. Once the horse was inside the city, they came out and conquered Troy.

▲ **A CASTLE FROM THE CRUSADES**
This 12th-century castle is on the southern coast of Turkey. It was used by knights during the Crusades.

The Turks and the Ottomans

The Roman Empire was also called the Byzantine Empire. In A.D. 1071, a group of people from the east called the Seljuk Turks captured the Byzantine land. The Seljuk Turks were Muslims, followers of the religion of Islam. The Byzantines were Christians. The Seljuks' victory upset Christians in Europe. A series of wars called the Crusades began. In the Crusades, large numbers of Christian soldiers and knights came from Europe. They fought the Muslim Seljuk Turks. They wanted to capture the region and return it to Christian rule.

In 1453, a Turkish nation called the Ottoman Empire captured Constantinople. It became one of the largest empires ever. It included European countries like Hungary, Bulgaria, and Yugoslavia. Where the Ottoman Empire did not rule directly, it usually had **trading outposts**. It was a huge and powerful empire.

▲ **TURKEY'S MOST FAMOUS LEADER**
Kemal Atatürk helped Turkey become independent from Greece. Above, a statue of Atatürk honors his bravery.

The Turkish Republic

The Ottoman Empire lasted into the 20th century. In 1914, the Ottomans sided with Germany in World War I. When the Germans and Turks lost the war in 1918, the Ottoman Empire was divided up. Most of Turkey was given to Greece, their ancient enemy.

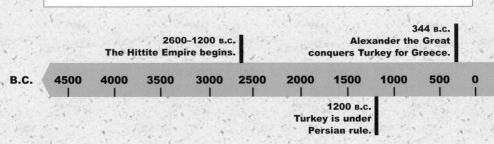

2600–1200 B.C.
The Hittite Empire begins.

344 B.C.
Alexander the Great
conquers Turkey for Greece.

B.C. | 4500 4000 3500 3000 2500 2000 1500 1000 500 0

1200 B.C.
Turkey is under
Persian rule.

The Turks fought to rid their country of the Greeks. By 1922, the Turks had mostly defeated them. In 1923, they signed a **treaty** and modern Turkey was born.

Atatürk

During the war of independence, a man named Kemal Atatürk took charge. After the war, he became Turkey's leader. Atatürk set about to reform Turkey and to make it a secular nation—secular means the government is nonreligious. Atatürk allowed the Turks freedom to practice any religion. He **abolished** many religious requirements. Women no longer had to wear veils. Men were not allowed to have more than one wife. Also, a western-style alphabet was adopted.

Many people wanted Turkey's government to remain Muslim. Other people praised Atatürk. They said it was fine to be Muslim, but that religion and government should be separate. Today, this debate still continues.

Atatürk died in 1938. Since his death, Turkey has had several small **revolutions**. However, it has always returned to a democratic form of government. Today Turkey is doing well. Its long history has also made this country a great place to visit and explore.

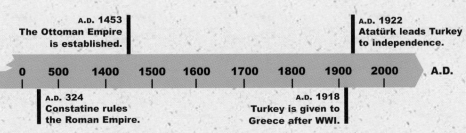

A.D. 1453
The Ottoman Empire
is established.

A.D. 1922
Atatürk leads Turkey
to independence.

0   500   1400   1500   1600   1700   1800   1900   2000   A.D.

A.D. 324
Constatine rules
the Roman Empire.

A.D. 1918
Turkey is given to
Greece after WWI.

A LOOK AT TURKEY'S GEOGRAPHY

Turkey is filled with mountains, deserts, canyons, and just about every other landscape you can think of. While you are there, take some time to relax by the ocean. Turkey has fabulous beaches. Read on to find out why Turkey is such a great place to visit.

Land

There are four different geographical regions in Turkey. The first is the low-lying coastal region in the north. A coastal region is an area that borders the sea, like a beach. These northern **plains** border on the Black Sea.

The second is the coastal region to the west. It lies along the Mediterranean Sea. This area is **fertile** and hot. It produces more food than any other in Turkey.

The southern coastal region is the third. This area also borders on the Mediterranean. It is a fertile area, but it is hotter and drier than the western coast.

The fourth region consists of the vast central uplands, sometimes divided into the western and eastern **plateaus**. This area is high, rocky, and dry. Two mountain ranges border this central area. To the north are the Pontic Mountains. To the south lie the Taurus Mountains. Turkey's highest peak is Mount Ararat, which stands at 16,849 feet (about 5,137 m). It is located near Turkey's border with Iran.

TURKEY'S SIZE ▶
Turkey is a very large country. It covers about 304,000 square miles (790,500 sq km). Turkey borders on several other nations, including Greece, Bulgaria, Syria, Iraq, Georgia, Armenia, and Iran.

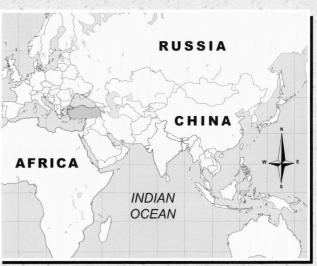

11

Water

Turkey borders on two major bodies of water, the Black Sea and the Mediterranean Sea. The part of the Mediterranean Sea to the west of Turkey is also called the Aegean Sea.

The most important body of water is the **channel** that connects the Black Sea to the Mediterranean. This area includes the Bosphorus **Straits** at the north. The larger Sea of Marmara is southwest of that. Farther west of the channel are straits called the Dardanelles. This channel provides a very important trade route for Turkey's neighbors to sail back and forth from the Black Sea to the Mediterranean Sea. Throughout history, whoever controlled this channel charged ships money to pass through it and gained a lot of power. Turkey's control of the area has made the country very powerful.

▲ SALT POOLS AT PUMUKKALE
Pumukkale means the "The Cotton Fortress."
The white walls and pools formed naturally from salt.
Visitors enjoy relaxing in the water.

Weather

Turkey is a very large country, and its **climate** changes from region to region. The mountainous northeast is the coldest part of the country. In winter, the temperature can fall to 40 degrees below zero Fahrenheit (-4° C). On the western Mediterranean coast, the temperatures rise into the 90s during the summer.

Istanbul is cooled by summer breezes—average high temperatures there reach only the low 80s Fahrenheit (27° C). In winter, average highs are in the 40s (4° C). In Istanbul's rainiest months, about 5 inches (13 cm) of rain falls. In drier months only about 1 inch (2.5 cm) falls.

The wettest area in Turkey is the western part of the Black Sea region. The yearly rainfall there is about 90 inches (229 cm)!

▲ **CLIMBING MOUNT ARARAT'S SNOWY PEAKS**
Above, climbers risk the dangers of Mount Ararat, Turkey's highest mountain. They wear heavy clothing to stay warm.

▲ **AT HOME IN THE VALLEY**
It is much warmer down in the valley than at the top of these mountains, which may be 15,000 feet high.

ISTANBUL: A BIG-CITY SNAPSHOT

▲ **TRAFFIC JAM IN ISTANBUL**
Busy and modern, the city of Istanbul has its share of traffic jams.

Istanbul is one of the biggest and most exciting cities in the world. The ancient city, first known as Byzantium and then called Constantinople, bridges two **continents**. A trip across the Bosphorus Bridge will take you from Europe to Asia! For hundreds of years Istanbul has been a place where different cultures have met, traded, and lived together. It remains this way today.

Above the Golden Horn

Start your tour on the European side of the city, north of the Golden Horn. The Golden Horn is a natural **harbor** cut into the land. It divides the European part of Istanbul in two. The best way to view this part of the city is by walking. Be sure to stop by the Dolma Bahçe Palace. Sultan Abdül Mecit built this palace in the early 19th century in the European style. It has marble walls, **chandeliers**, and winding staircases.

Next, head to the shopping area called Balîk Pazar. You can shop in the book stores and **antique** stalls—you might find a treasure! The Balîk Pazar is also a great place to have lunch. Order a doner kabap (something like a lamb sandwich) from one of the stands. It is delicious.

Beneath the Golden Horn

In this area you will many interesting places to visit. One highlight is the Aya Sofya. A Byzantine emperor built this as a Christian church 1,500 years ago. It was converted into a Muslim **mosque** and later into a museum.

The Blue Mosque is one of the most beautiful mosques in the world. It was built in the early 17th century. Its huge domes and towers will amaze you. Inside, the **mosaic** tile and stonework were made with awesome detail.

The Grand Bazaar is found to the northwest of the Blue Mosque. If you need anything—from toothpaste to exotic jewelry or fabulous Turkish carpets—this is the place to find it. Thousands of stalls line this Middle Eastern shopping mall. It is a shopper's paradise.

Finish your tour beneath the Golden Horn at the Turkish and Islamic Arts Museum. There you can learn about many of the arts and crafts you have seen.

Across the Bosphorus

Are you ready to leave the continent of Europe? You can cross into Asia over the Bosphorus Bridge. If you like stories of ancient battles, head to the Andalou Hisarî, just outside of Üsküdar. This fortress was built at the end of the 14th century. Ottoman military leaders planned part of their invasion of Constantinople from here.

To finish your tour of Istanbul, head to Büyük Çamlica, a park that sits high on a hill above the city. It is a great spot to snap some photos or have a picnic.

SAINT SOPHIA'S CHURCH ▶
The Hagia Sophia, called the Aya Sofya in Turkish, was built as a church about 1,700 years ago. Today, it serves as a history museum.

ISTANBUL'S TOP-10 CHECKLIST

If you visit Istanbul, here's a list of the top 10 things to do.

☐ Discover how Ottoman rulers lived at Dolma Bahçe Palace.

☐ Have a doner kabap and lemonade for lunch at the Balik Pazar.

☐ Wander the garden of Topkapi Palace.

☐ Visit the Aya Sofya. Remember, this building is about 1,700 years old!

☐ Head to the Blue Mosque and snap some photos.

☐ Go shopping in the Grand Bazaar for... everything!

☐ Learn about ancient Turkish arts at the Turkish and Islamic Arts Museum.

☐ Have dinner in downtown Üsküdar, in the Asian part of the city.

☐ Tour the fortress of Andalou Hisarî.

☐ Watch the sun set from Büyük Çamlica, a park overlooking Istanbul.

4 TOP SIGHTS

Do you want to see it all on your trip to Turkey? It may be hard to decide where to start. Here are four places you won't want to miss—Ankara, Nemrut Dagî, Ephesus, and Hattuøa.

Ankara

Ankara is Turkey's capital and the center of Turkey's government. About 80 years ago, only 30,000 people lived there. Today it is home to nearly four million people. Most of Ankara's buildings are new and modern.

But some wonderful buildings are very, very old. One is the castle called the Ankara Kalesi. This ancient fort was constructed by a Byzantine emperor in the 800s.

For a wealth of information about Turkey's ancient history, visit Ankara's Museum of Anatolian Civilization. It's the best place to learn why Turkey has also been called the land of Byzantium, the Ottoman Empire, and Anatolia.

You should also visit Kemal Atatürk's **tomb**. Atatürk founded the Turkish Republic (see the chapter on Turkey's history for more information). Atatürk spent all his time in Ankara when he was the leader of Turkey. Today his tomb is guarded by the Turkish military. It is decorated with bronze doors and marble.

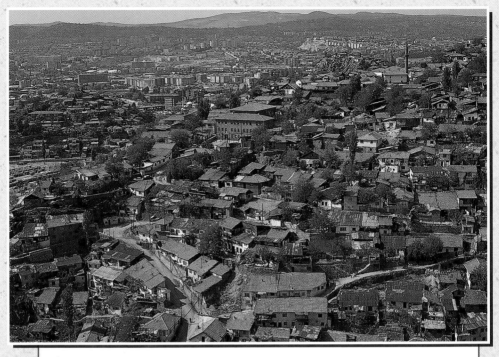

▲ **OVERLOOKING ANKARA**
This view of Ankara, Turkey's capital, is from a building called the Citadel.

◄ **ATATÜRK'S TOMB**
The White Guard protects Atatürk's tomb. Many Turkish ceremonies are held here.

▲ OFF WITH THEIR HEADS!
At Nemrut Dagî, the heads of giant statues lie on the ground. Built around 40 B.C. for King Antiochus I, Nemrut Dagî sits at the top of Mount Nemrut.

Nemrut Dagî

Your fourth fabulous Turkish sight is Nemrut Dagî in the east. It is a burial monument and temple left behind by King Antiochus of Persia in 40 B.C. He wanted everyone to remember him after he died. He put up large statues of gods that surround a huge statue of himself. Many of the statues were broken over the years. The heads of the statues lie on the ground next to their bodies. The heads alone are about 7 feet (2 m) high!

Interestingly, this monument was forgotten until 1881, when a scientist accidentally stumbled upon it. Today Nemrut Dagî is one Turkey's most popular tourist attractions.

FASCINATING FACT

Over the years, very strong earthquakes have rocked Turkey. They have caused thousands of deaths. The earthquakes also beheaded the statues at Nemrut Dagî. The statues' heads often lie next to their bodies. Talk about losing your head!

Ephesus

This ancient city on the Mediterranean Sea began around 600 B.C. No one lives there now. Over the years, many civilizations and emperors claimed it, including Alexander the Great. The Romans, however, are responsible for what remains there today.

Ephesus once served as the capital of the Roman **province** called Asia. It grew rich through trading. A lot of this money was used to construct buildings. The buildings of Ephesus were some of the most beautiful in the ancient world, and you can see them—or parts of them—today. Take your time to wander under all the ancient arches and carved stone gateways. It is worth spending a whole day there.

One of the highlights of Ephesus is the Great Theater. This theater actually dates back to before the Romans came, around 300 B.C. The Romans expanded the stage and added a huge stone backdrop. The theater can seat 25,000 people! It is still used today.

You should also check out the remains of the library at Ephesus. This building used to house scrolls. Scrolls are long, rolled-up sheets of paper with writing on them—they were used before books. This library once held 12,000 scrolls. It was one of the largest libraries in the world.

ROMAN BRICK ROAD ▶
Visitors explore the
remains of Ephesus,
once a very important
city in the Roman
Empire.

▲ **CELCUS LIBRARY**
Long ago, this library was one of the largest in the world.
It was built around the year A.D. 114.

▲ **HITTITE EMPIRE**
Hattuøa was once the capital of the Hittite Empire. The great stone walls helped protect the city—4,000 years ago.

◄ **TURKISH DOLLS**
Handmade Turkish dolls make nice souvenirs.

Hattuøa

Many different kingdoms once ruled Turkey. One civilization you should not forget about is the Hittite Empire. This ancient kingdom was huge. One of its main cities was Hattuøa.

Like Ephesus, Hattuøa is now deserted—no one lives there. All that is left are ruins. Exotic temples, secret tunnels, and neat burial sites fill the city. The Aslanî Kapî, or Lion's Gate, is a great way to enter the city walls. The two stone lions at this gate were believed to protect the city. The walls near the Lion's Gate stretch for nearly 4 miles (6.4 km). They were built 4,000 years ago.

Be sure to tour the fortress called Büyük Kale. This enormous fort was where Hittite **nobility** lived and worked. The Büyük Kale's walls are **inscribed** with hieroglyphics, an ancient form of writing that uses pictures for words. You will also find drawings and carvings.

Hattuøa is also home to the ruins of the Büyük Mabed, the Great Temple of the Storm God. This temple was built in the 1300s B.C. It honored the Hittites' most important god.

GOING TO SCHOOL IN TURKEY

Turkish children are supposed to go to school for at least five years. This is not always possible for families who live far from cities, but most Turks do get some education. After five years of elementary school, when students are about 12 years old, they can choose to continue in school, or can go to work. If a student continues, school is free.

Students who continue with education go to middle school for three years. Those who go on after middle school either do a three-year college-preparatory program or go to a vocational school. Vocational schools teach the skills needed to do certain types of jobs.

Turkey has 29 universities. Students attend them after the college-preparatory program. The University of Istanbul is one of the oldest schools in the world. It was founded in A.D. 1453.

◄ A TURKISH CLASSROOM
Two students study hard in this all-girls school. They learn many of the same subjects as you do.

Turkey's most popular sport is soccer. Most cities have teams that compete with other teams around the country. Turkey is famous for its soccer fans.

Turks have their very own brand of wrestling. It is a little unusual to foreigners, but people in Turkey love it. Basically, two men put on leather pants and grease themselves up with olive oil. Then they wrestle. The challenge is to pin your slippery opponent down. The ancient Greeks wrestled the same way 3,000 years ago!

▲ CAMEL WRESTLING
Camel wrestling is also quite popular. The camels wear muzzles so they cannot bite. If one camel gets too rough, the pair is separated. No one wants to let the camels get hurt.

FROM FARMING TO FACTORIES

Turkey produces more food than it needs. Its huge farmlands grow wheat, barley, sugar beets, and other products that it sells around the world. The most fertile farmlands are along the Mediterranean coast. There, farmers grow vegetables and fruit, and raise animals like sheep and goats.

Many Turks work in factories. Turkish factories make automobiles, electronics, and chemicals. They also make food products for sale around the world. Another important industry in Turkey is tobacco. Turks grow huge amounts of tobacco. They use it to make cigarettes and other tobacco products.

Another way many Turks make a living is through tourism. Turkey is a popular place to visit, and every tourist brings money to the country. All those visitors pay for hotels, meals, and entrance fees to historical sights. In addition, Turks make a living doing the things that keep any society running. They are doctors, lawyers, cab drivers, shop owners, and so on.

The kind of money used in Turkey is called the Turkish lira. When people buy things there, they pay using the Turkish lira.

▲ GRAND BAZAAR
The Grand Bazaar is a covered market in Istanbul. It sells dishes, jewelry, and other treasures.

SORTING APRICOTS ▶
An apricot is a small orange fruit that looks like a peach. Apricots are an important crop in Turkey.

THE TURKISH GOVERNMENT

Turkey is a democracy. That means Turkish people vote to elect their leaders. Turkey has a president, a prime minister, and a Grand National Assembly, which has 550 members. They meet in Ankara, the capital.

The people elect the members of the Grand National Assembly. Members serve five-year terms. The Grand National Assembly is in charge of making the country's laws. It also has another important function—choosing the president.

The president of Turkey is the head of the army. He or she also approves the laws passed by the Grand National Assembly. In addition, the president chooses the prime minister.

Turkey's prime minister works with the Grand National Assembly to make the country's laws. The prime minister also appoints other ministers to help with this task.

TURKEY'S NATIONAL FLAG

The Turkish flag is red with a white crescent moon and a star. These are ancient symbols of both Islam and the Ottoman Empire. The flag was an Islamic green color but after the declaration of the republic, the color was changed back to red.

RELIGIONS OF TURKEY

Almost 98% of all Turkish people are Muslim. Muslims are people who practice the religion of Islam. They follow the teachings of Mohammed, found in a holy book called the Koran.

Although most people in Turkey practice Islam, there is no official religion. People in Turkey are allowed to practice whatever religion they wish—this is called freedom of religion. Many Muslims in Turkey today would like the country to have an official religion. Others are happy keeping government and religion separate—which is called the separation of church and state. These two different opinions are often important in **political campaigns**.

A small number of Turkish people practice Christianity. Christians follow the teachings of Jesus, found in the New Testament of the Bible. Some Jewish people live in Turkey, as well. They observe the teachings of the Torah, which is also known as the Old Testament of the Bible.

SULEYMAN MOSQUE ▶
A mosque is a building where Muslims gather to pray. This one is decorated with 20,000 blue tiles.

TURKISH FOOD

One important word you will need to know if you go to Turkey is "dolma." It means two things. First, a dolma is a stuffed vegetable. It is filled with things like pine nuts, rice, and meat. Second, a dolma is a kind of public taxicab! Taxis were named this because there are often so many people packed into a Turkish cab it feels like being stuffed into a vegetable.

The dolma is one of the most popular foods in Turkey, but it is only one of many things you will find on a Turkish table. The main meat Turks eat is lamb. They also eat some chicken and fish. Turks usually cook meat on a stick, or minced and formed into something like meatballs. Turks eat meat with rice, thin, flat bread, and plenty of vegetables. Eggplant is one of the most popular vegetables in Turkey.

Turks eat lots of pastries, cookies, and cakes for dessert. Baklava is one of the most famous Turkish desserts. It is made from thin dough, pistachios, honey, and pine nuts. If you make it to Turkey, be sure to try some baklava. It is sticky and sweet—and delicious.

◀ **TURKISH TEATIME**
A traditional Turkish tea set. In Turkey, taking a tea break is a popular way to relax with friends.

Turkey's Recipe

TURKISH LEMONADE

Ingredients:

3 cups plus 3 tbsp sugar

12 cups water

4 tsp lemon rind

24 sprigs mint

12 medium lemons

WARNING:
Never cook or bake by yourself.
Always have an adult assist you
in the kitchen.

Directions:

Mix three cups of sugar with 12 cups of water. Roll together 20

mint leaves with the lemon rind and 3 tablespoons of sugar

(the sugar brings out the flavor of the mint and the lemon rind).

Add the sugar, mint, and lemon rind mixture to the water. Squeeze

the lemons to make lemon juice. Add the lemon juice to the water

mixture. Serve very cold with mint sprigs.

UP CLOSE: CAPPADOCIA

After Istanbul, Cappadocia should probably be at the top of your list of places to visit in Turkey. Thousands of years ago, people discovered that the rock walls of Cappadocia's cliffs and canyons in eastern Turkey were soft enough to carve. Ever since, people have built their homes by **burrowing** directly into the rock walls. Some of these homes are simple one-room dwellings. Others are the size of small palaces. In fact, entire cities have been carved into the rock! Do you want to learn more about this incredible place? Read on.

Göreme

The city of Göreme has many of the rock dwellings that make Cappadocia famous. Göreme hosts the huge Open-Air Museum. You have to pay to enter the area, but it's worth it. You can spend hours climbing ancient staircases, wandering along the cliffs, and passing in and out of the rock. The coolest parts are the churches. Small passageways give way to huge chapels and sleeping quarters.

Make sure to visit the Dark Church, called Karanlîk Kilise in Turkish. This buried church is famous for its frescoes, which are paintings made on a plaster wall. The frescoes date back to the 11th century. Also be sure to check out the Elmalî Kilise, or Apple Church. This church is also famous for its frescoes. Finally, head to the Göreme National Park to view the area's natural beauty.

▼ GÖREME

Hundreds of homes and churches are carved into this mountain. These buildings are fun to explore—no one lives there anymore.

CLAY POTTERY ▶

This potter makes beautifully decorated vases and dishes to sell. His family business is four generations old.

▲ UNDERGROUND CITY
When wars broke out above ground, villagers hid in cities under the ground. They traveled through narrow passages like the one above, in Cappadocia.

Derinkuyu

Over the past 3,000 years, Turkey has had some violent wars. When war broke out, it was best to hide underground. The people of entire villages would disappear beneath the ground. Sometimes they stayed there for months at a time.

There are nearly 30 underground cities in Cappadocia. Some historians believe they first appeared about 2,000 B.C. One of these cities is Derinkuyu. The rooms in Derinkuyu stretch across eight underground levels. You may get tired climbing all the stairs—there were no elevators in ancient times.

Most of the rooms are empty. You will see kitchens, bedrooms, and common areas where people spent time together, or you may even wander into a room that was used to house animals.

The caves are cool and dark. There is no natural light. Lanterns hang from the walls to help you find your way. Be sure you stay with your tour guide on the marked path. You definitely don't want to get lost in this maze of tunnels.

HOLIDAYS

People in Turkey celebrate many national and religious holidays. Republic Day is a national holiday that falls on October 29. It celebrates the start of the Turkish Republic in 1923.

Since most Turks practice Islam, many people observe Islamic religious holidays. During the month-long holiday of Ramadan, Muslims **fast** during the day. They eat large dinners after the sun goes down. Ramadan Bayramî marks the end of Ramadan, when Muslims return to eating during the day.

The most important Muslim holiday in Turkey is Kurban Bayramî. It celebrates an event in the Old Testament of the Bible. About 2.5 million lambs are slaughtered in Turkey during this holiday, which lasts for about five days. During Kurban Bayramî, people visit family and friends to feast on the lamb.

◀ YOUTH DAY
On May 19, Turkey celebrates Youth Day to remember the beginning of the War of Independence. Children are honored because they will carry on Turkey's freedom.

LEARNING THE LANGUAGE

English	Turkish	How to say it
Hello	Merhaba	MER-ha-ba
My name is _____	Benim Adim_____	BEH-nihm ah-DUHM
Thank you	Teflekkür ederim	TEFF-luh-KOORR EH-DHER-uhm
What time is it?	Saat kac?	SAAHT KAHCH?
Where are you from?	Nerelisiniz	NEH-rehl his-IHN-ihz

QUICK FACTS

TURKEY

Capital ▶
Ankara

Borders
Black Sea (N)
Georgia and Armenia (NE)
Iran (E)
Iraq, Syria,
Mediterranean Sea (S)
Aegean Sea, Greece (W)
Bulgaria (NW)

Area
301,382 square miles
(780,580 sq km)

Population
67,308,928

▼ **Largest Cities**
Istanbul (10,250,000 people)
Ankara (2,890,025)
Izmir (1,920,807)
Adana (1,010,363)
Bursa (949,810)

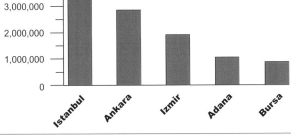

▲ Flag of Turkey

Longest River
Kizil Irmak, 715 miles long
(1,150 km)

Coastline ▶
4,471 miles (7,200 km)

Literacy Rate
81% of all Turkish people
can read

Major Industries
Textiles, food processing,
mining (coal, chromite,
copper, boron, minerals)

Chief Crops
Cotton, tobacco, grain, olives,
sugar beets, pulses, citrus,
livestock

Natural Resources
Antimony, coal, chromium,
mercury, copper, boron,
minerals

◀ Monetary Unit
Turkish Lira

43

PEOPLE TO KNOW

◀ TANSU ÇILLER

Tansu Çiller is one of the leaders of Turkey's True Path Party. In 1993, she became Turkey's first female prime minister. She later lost reelection, but still serves in Turkey's government. She was born in 1946.

KEMAL ATATÜRK ▶

Kemal Atatürk was the founder of modern Turkey. He began many reforms. He brought independence to Turkey, he gave women the right to vote, and he allowed freedom of religion. He was born in 1881 and died in 1938.

◀ SEZEN AKSU

This is one of Turkey's favorite pop stars. She's known for her great voice and her loud excited fans. If Turkey has a Britney Spears, Sezen Aksu is it.

MORE TO READ

Want to know more about Turkey? Take a look at some of the books below.

Bator, Robert and Rothero, Chris. *Daily Life in Ancient and Modern Istanbul*. Minneapolis, MN: Lerner Publishing Group, 2000.
Learn the history of Istanbul and what it is like to live in this ancient city.

Feinstein, Steve, et al. *Turkey in Pictures*. Minneapolis, MN: Lerner Publishing Group, 1998.
Explore Turkey through beautiful, full-color photos.

Green, Roger Lancelyn. *A Tale of Troy*. New York, NY: Puffin, 1995.
Tells the tale of the Trojan Horse and gives the background of the story.

Sheehan, Sean. *Turkey*. Tarrytown, NY: Marshall Cavendish, 1996.
A good resource for additional information on this fascinating country.

Spencer, William. *The Lands and People of Turkey*. New York: HarperCollins Children's Books, 1989.
Discover the different cultures and lifestyles of the various regions of Turkey.

GLOSSARY

Abolished (uh-BOHL-isht)—put an end to

Antique (an-TEEK)—very old, usually more than 100 years

Burrowing (BUR-oh-ing)—making a hole or tunnel in the ground

Chandeliers (shan-duh-LEERZ)—very fancy light fixtures

Channel (CHAN-uhl)—a passageway dug for water

Climate (KLY-miht)—the weather conditions in a place

Continents (KAHN-tih-nentz)—the seven largest bodies of land on Earth (Africa, Antarctica, Asia, Australia, Europe, North America, South America)

Empire (EM-pire)—a number of countries joined together under one ruler

Exotic (ex-AH-tik)—strange or unusual in style

Fast (FAST)—a period of time when a person chooses not to eat

Fertile (FUR-tihl)—full of nutrients, good for growing crops

Harbor (HAR-bur)—a quiet, sheltered part of a sea where ships can be safe

Metropolis (meh-TROP-uh-lihs)—a large city

Mosque (MOSK)—the building where Muslims pray

Nobility (noh-BILL-uh-tee)—people who have a high rank in society, such as princes and dukes

Plains (PLAYNZ)—wide open lands with few big trees

Plateaus (pla-TOEZ)—high, level lands

Political campaigns (puh-LIT-ih-kuhl cam-PAINZ)—the speeches, personal appearances, and advertising of people who are running for office

Province (PRAH-vince)—a part of a country, similar to a state

Reforms (reh-FORMZ)—changes that make a government more honest, often leading to better living conditions for everyone

Revolutions (rev-oh-LOO-shunz)—uprisings by the people of a country to change its government

Straits (STRATES)—very narrow bodies of water that connect two other bodies of water

Sultans (SUHL-tuhnz)—the kings of Turkey and some other Muslim lands

Tomb (TOOM)—a small building over a grave

Trading outposts (TRAY-ding OUT-pohsts)—markets in faraway places where goods are bought and sold, or traded

Treaty (TREE-tee)—a written agreement between two countries to end a war and have normal relations

INDEX